GRACE HAPPENS AGAIN

Don Knudson

Cartoons by Ray Johnson

PLEASE RETURN TO:

Barb Keller
17330 Ipswich Way
Lakeville, MN 55044

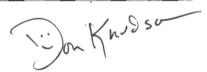

HPA

Publishing consultant: Huff Publishing Associates, LLC
www.huffpublishing.com

Cartoons by Ray Johnson

Cover and interior design by Marti Naughton

Printed in the United States of America
ISBN 978-0-9895277-9-8

Ray's ordination 1968

Ray at age sixty-one

As a reader of this book, I want you to know about Ray Johnson: his life, work, and struggles. As his friend and "brother," I created this book using his cartoons and my reflections to celebrate his legacy and share it more widely.

Ray was born in Munising, Michigan, and lived there until after high school when he attended art school in Chicago, Illinois. His family of origin was of modest means. His father worked for the paper mill, and the family lived in a house provided by the mill. This Finnish family attended a small Suomi Synod Lutheran church that in 1963 joined the Free Lutheran denomination. According to family, Ray's mother was told by *her* family that she was going to hell because she left the Apostolic Lutheran Church to marry his father. This condemnation lasted until her dying day. Ray's father was also socially conservative and unbending. Ray's conservative upbringing later became a source of friction between him and his parents, especially with his father.

After attending art school in Chicago, Ray earned a bachelor's degree in social work at Michigan State and then went to Northwestern Lutheran Seminary in St. Paul, Minnesota, which is where I met Ray.

Thanks to the support and encouragement of many friends—who were also friends of Ray—who helped make this book possible, especially to John Johnson and other of his seminary classmates. Ray's widow and family have been gracious to support this effort. I thank my wife Gloria Swanson for her supporting me in creating this book. I could not have done this without Bill Huff of Huff Publishing who listened to what I wanted to do and encouraged me. And I thank Susan Niemi who works with Bill as editor, who took my script and made it fun to read. And most of all I am grateful for the grace of God that has allowed me to live through the darkest days of my depression to join up and reconnect with Ray. My life was renewed and blessed because of our relationship. I miss him deeply. May his heavenly Father forever listen to his sermons and laugh at his cartoons. That's really all he ever wanted or needed.

Don Knudson

Introduction

Ray Johnson and I were seminarians together during the late 1960s. The civil rights movement and the Vietnam War had society in turmoil. Bob Dylan famously declared, "The times they are a-changin'." We were on our launch pad at seminary being trained for ordained ministry in the Lutheran church while astronauts at NASA were on their launch pad practicing to orbit the moon and put a man there for the first time in history. It was an exciting time to be alive.

For Ray, seminary was the best of times. There his world view widened, his intellect blossomed, and his love for social justice developed. This led to further strain between Ray and his father. Ray told me several times after he was ordained that when his father visited he refused to attended Ray's church or to hear him preach. He carried the wound of a critical and disapproving father all his life.

Ray was called and ordained to be pastor of St. Peter's Lutheran Church in New York Mills, Minnesota, in 1968. He served there for more than seventeen years. I joined him in 1970 as a fellow pastor in the Red River Valley Synod of the Lutheran Church in America. The synod geographically covered North and South Dakota and northwest Minnesota. During that period of time Pastor Ron Gladen was an assistant to the bishop. He saw Ray at synod gatherings and pastoral retreats drawing cartoons, expressing his views, editorializing in response to a speaker, or just simply making a humorous statement. Pastor Gladen said, "One of the best decisions I made as editor of the Red River Valley Synod's monthly newspaper was to ask Ray to provide a monthly editorial cartoon. Not only were his cartoons insightful and timely for our readers, but in the annual rating of all synod newspapers, I could count on at least one first place every year for Best Editorial Cartoon."

During those years, Ray was married to Ruth Olson. Together they adopted two special needs sons, Aaron and Nate. As the children grew, the challenges and struggles with meeting the children's special needs increased. Ray eventually took a call to a church in Billings, Montana. There he experienced a major crisis resulting in the breakup of his marriage and family. Ray fell into deep depression and was hospitalized. The trauma of his family breakup left Ray facing years of struggle. He moved back to Minneapolis to recover. And that's where we found each other again. Through those same years I had had my own struggles with stress and depression and was also hospitalized. My first marriage of twenty-four years to Eline Grosfield also ended; we had two children, Karla and Kristin. Divorce had not been on my list of things to do.

When we were ordained, our bishop had made it clear that any pastor who divorced had also lost the right to be a pastor. This judgment heightened my sense of failure, adding to my depression as it had for Ray. So here we were, two Lutheran pastors, both chewed up by stress and depression with nothing to brag about. Times may have softened the stigma of depression in the past twenty years, but suffering depression as a pastor is nothing you want to put on your resume. The experience with failure and deep despair led us to seek support and mutual understanding. The illness, I believe, deepened us spiritually, no more going it alone. We pledged to each other that we would be brothers. And brothers we became! He was there for me, and I was there for him.

Our lives moved on. In 1997 I met and married Gloria Swanson, and Ray later met and married Donna Divine. We continued our mutual support of each other as brothers until his untimely and sudden death on July 25, 2005. In Donna's words: "I met Ray in 2000 when he was fifty-nine. We married in 2001, and he died in 2005 at age sixty-five. We were happy together. You know that part," she says to me, "but I like saying it." And it was true, and it was divine!

Donna recounts that "Ray never had a lot of money, but he was accomplished in many areas besides ministry. He was an athlete who loved biking, downhill skiing, in-line skating, and sail boating. He was a marathon runner and loved playing tennis. Ray was a painter, poet, cartoonist, craftsman, gardener, and model boat and model railroad builder." He was all of that even as he carried the burden of an unrelenting mood of depression.

When Ray and I would get together for support he always had a sketch pad with his latest cartoons. As he showed me what he'd drawn, it amazed me how he'd captured the ironies and the foibles of religious community and daily life. Seeing Ray's cartoons helped me laugh. When I was diagnosed with prostate cancer, Ray drew several humorous cartoons making fun with me over a serious situation. That was Ray!

For Ray, humor was grace. The fact is all of us live through times of failure, deep sadness, and loss. We all need humor to bring us grace and perspective. Ray created the almost famous Grace Happens bumper sticker while working with the Crossroads Ministry, a community outreach program at Augustana Lutheran Church, Minneapolis, Minnesota. Indeed, grace does happen.

Now that you know more about Ray, I hope the pages of this book will help you laugh, and wonder, and think, and question what is important in life. If you had a hard landing, a setback, a series of tragic losses, then you know pain and struggle. Seek support and help. For *Grace Happens* unexpectedly, as a gift. It matters not how dark the gloom. I can hear Ray saying to me now, "We both needed a dash of humor and grace."

Pastor Don Knudson, MDiv, BCC

Blessing and curse

The Lord spoke to Moses, saying: Speak to Aaron and his sons, saying, Thus you shall bless the Israelites: You shall say to them, The Lord bless you and keep you; the Lord make his face to shine upon you, and be gracious to you; the Lord lift up his countenance upon you, and give you peace. So they shall put my name on the Israelites, and I will bless them. Numbers 6:22, 27

We begin the new year remembering the blessing Moses gave to Aaron and his sons with which to bless the Israelites. So God wishes to bless us also.

The experience of being blessed is a gift. Beginning a new year with a sense of blessing is ours to claim. It makes a difference in how we look at the world around us. In the northern climates where snow is part of life, we can view this part of nature in both a negative and positive way. Snow can be thought a curse or a blessing. When we think of struggling, slogging through and shoveling snow, it seems a curse. When we enjoy its beauty and anticipate a time of playing in the snow, then we are blessed.

Ray's cartoon expresses the playful side of winter's beauty. "Snow must be God's winter popcorn!" YES! It is wintertime! With what attitude do you approach wintertime?

With what blessings do you begin the new year? Name them and claim them. This is your life. This is your year to live with all the blessings God is giving you.

Help me see the blessings you have given me. Forgive me when my energy goes into negative and self-defeating behaviors. Help me to be renewed every day by your grace. Amen

Grow in wisdom and knowledge

For learning about wisdom and instruction, for understanding words of insight, for gaining instruction in wise dealing, righteousness, justice, and equity; to teach shrewdness to the simple, knowledge and prudence to the young—let the wise also hear and gain in learning, and the discerning acquire skill, to understand a proverb and a figure, the words of the wise and their riddles. The fear of the Lord is the beginning of knowledge; fools despise wisdom and instruction. *Proverbs 1:2-7 (the proverbs of Solomon son of David, king of Israel)*

The beginning of a new year is a good time to look back and reflect. Often our lives are too caught up in the next thing, and we don't take the time to pause, think, reflect, and review. I invite you to take a few moments now to reflect upon what has happened in your life. What major life experiences have you had this past year? What major milestones did you mark in your life? What challenges did you face? From the point in your life that you now enjoy, what lessons have you learned over the past year? What unfinished business are you carrying into the new year?

Notice the values mentioned in the text from Proverbs. Are these values present in your life as lived today? Are there values you wish to strengthen as you look forward to this new year? As the book of Proverbs advises, don't be a fool and despise wisdom and instruction. This is a great time to grow a deeper spiritual and meaningful life.

Lord, as long as we live and breathe we have opportunity to grow in wisdom and knowledge. Thank you for giving us this opportunity to learn. Amen

TURNUPS®

BY: RAY JOHNSON

The hidden revealed

No one after lighting a lamp hides it under a jar, or puts it under a bed, but puts it on a lampstand, so that those who enter may see the light. For nothing is hidden that will not be disclosed, nor is anything secret that will not become known and come to light. *Luke 8:16-17*

I have a confession to make. Sometimes when I get up early in the morning and my wife is still sleeping I try to not awaken her. So I get dressed for work in the dark. I do my best to choose the right clothes but sometimes when I come home after work my wife says, "That shirt doesn't go with those pants. You must have dressed in the dark!" I'm busted again! What happened in the dark is revealed in the light.

Sometimes we want to hide our mistakes and keep embarrassing or even illegal things hidden. It takes a lot of energy to cover up our failures and mistakes. Usually we find our efforts fail. Our life grows more complicated, and our pretensions leave us feeling isolated. Whatever problem we are trying to avoid becomes worse.

Christ came to bring light into the world. That means our sins are revealed. It is good spiritual practice to learn to accept our mistakes and to own up to our failings. Then we can discover the true life Christ brings.

Help me dig through the stuff in my life to get down to the real issues I face. Help me know that you see my failings, even when I don't see them myself. Yet you still love me. Thank you for accepting me the way I am. Amen

Your God too small?

As the prophet says, "Heaven is my throne, and the earth is my footstool. What kind of house will you build for me, says the Lord, or what is the place of my rest? Did not my hand make all these things?" Acts 7:48-50

As I entered the church sanctuary one Sunday morning dressed in my pastoral robe, a little child said to her mother, "Look, mommy, there's Jesus!" We all smiled at the young child's effort to comprehend God and Jesus. Ideas of God forged in the imaginations of small children are concrete and specific. For that child I was "Jesus" or "God." Yes there may be a small truth in what the child imagined. The pastor is called to reflect the image of God through preaching and sacraments, even though imperfectly. But God is much more.

What is your image, your imagination, of God? It may tell you a lot about what you learned as a child. Could God be much more than you imagine? J.B. Phillips wrote a book many years ago called *Your God Is Too Small.* He challenged the conventional and limiting images of God common among us. I believe most of our images of God are too small. God cannot be contained by temples built by hand or by the imaginations of our minds.

Lord, you are who you are. Forgive me when I try to confine you to the limits of my imagination. Wow me with your majesty and mystery. Amen

When Christ's appearing
Was made known
King Herod trembled
For his throne;
But He who offers
Heavenly birth
Seeks not the kingdom
Of this earth.

Christ revealed: Epiphany

In the time of King Herod, after Jesus was born in Bethlehem of Judea, wise men from the East came to Jerusalem, asking, "Where is the child who has been born king of the Jews? For we observed his star at its rising, and have come to pay him homage." When King Herod heard this, he was frightened, and all Jerusalem with him; and calling together all the chief priests and scribes of the people, he inquired of them where the Messiah was to be born. They told him, "In Bethlehem of Judea; for so it has been written by the prophet: 'And you, Bethlehem, in the land of Judah, are by no means least among the rulers of Judah; for from you shall come a ruler who is to shepherd my people Israel.'" *Matthew 2:1-6*

Epiphany of Our Lord is the day and season of the church year to recognize that the gospel is for all nations. Misunderstandings greeted the birth of Jesus as fears of the unknown haunted those in power. Herod, in particular, was fearful of losing his power.

A star shined forth to the wise men of the east. It brought to their attention that a child was born to be king of the Jews. The news was spreading. We see the first hint of purpose that reaches out to the whole world. Christ's kingdom would not be temporal but spiritual. It is shown as fulfillment of past hopes expressed by the prophets. The spiritual kingdom would intersect with the world, but it would not seek to be a worldly kingdom. The kingdom was meant for all peoples.

As you encounter the diversity of our society and world today, can you imagine a spirituality that is universal enough for everyone? Many religions have made universal claims yet they remain bound to a particular geography or culture. Can the universal message of Jesus succeed in the diversity and conflicting agendas of today's world?

Shine your light and salvation upon our hearts that we may see more clearly how we may be drawn together as human beings wherever we may live. Amen

The baptism of Jesus

And when Jesus also had been baptized and was praying, the heaven was opened, and the Holy Spirit descended upon him in bodily form like a dove. And a voice came from heaven, "You are my Son, the Beloved; with you I am well pleased." *Luke 3:21-22*

The baptism of Jesus was the occasion when God's Spirit made public declaration of Christ's identity as God's beloved Son. His public ministry was revealed. The baptism Jesus received was the baptism of John, who called for repentance in preparation for the coming of the Lord. This was not yet what we call Christian baptism. It was an act of preparation. John was preparing the way, paving the way of salvation for the one who was coming.

When Luke's gospel tells the story it is to show that Jesus embraces the ministry of John the Baptist and his message. In the midst of this submission, Jesus is revealed by the voice from heaven as the Son of God with whom God is well pleased.

From this time forward in reading this gospel, we know who Jesus is. His actions and ministry are from God. The call for repentance has begun and will continue as God reveals God's purpose and intention for the world.

As Christians, we are brought into relationship with Jesus, Son of God, through Christian baptism. Like John before Jesus, we are ritually washed and cleansed from sin. From this time forward our lives are lived with repentance dependent on faith in Jesus Christ. We are marked with the cross of Christ. This gives us identity, too. We are now children of God. We belong to the way of renewal and salvation. How do you remember and celebrate your baptism?

Remembering the baptism of Jesus, we also remember our own baptism and identity as children of God. Help us walk the way of repentance and forgiveness. Amen

God's love for the environment

Your steadfast love, O Lord, extends to the heavens, your faithfulness to the clouds. Psalm 36:5

When we are born, we awaken in a world that has been here long before we became conscious or curious. Under the guidance and direction of our parents we explore that world as small children, learning about the laws of physics as we run and fall, drop things, bump into hard objects, and experience pain. We delight in new flavors and the smell of food and flowers. We look out and discover trees, mountains, plains, plants, and animals of every kind.

The environment is a gift of love. It has favored the existence of life and in particular, now, our own personal lives. The existence of our planet and its natural wonders is a source of surprise and amazement. The psalmist connects the steadfast love of God to the heavens and to the clouds.

Astronomers are looking to see if there is anything else in the universe like us. As they look up they see back in time. They have discovered a universe very amazing and strange, far exceeding anyone's wildest imagination. Images from the Hubble telescope have opened our eyes to millions of galaxies and uncountable stars.

Among other things, astronomers are looking for other planets where life may exist. Are we alone? Is life possible elsewhere? Some evidence already gives hints of possible planetary life. Watery planets are being sought using telescopes applying many ingenious strategies to discover clues of life in another planetary world. Time and effort will reveal what is possible to discover. But for us, there's no doubt our earth is the only one we have.

The experience of being alive and conscious on this planet is astonishing. Our curiosity wonders where there might be other places like our earth. For those of us who have not looked through a telescope, it is still possible to use our capacity for curiosity and wonder. Just look out of the window, scan the sky, and look at the birds. See the snowdrifts with the tracks of rabbits and deer. And in summer take in the beauty of flowers.

It will take your breath away when you realize the amazing gift of love it is to be alive, breathing the air around you. We live and move and have our being in this amazing environment: God's gift of love to each one of us. It is ours to enjoy, ours to respect, and ours to protect. How do you think we are doing?

With eyes I see the wonders of sky, land, and seas. I smell the fresh wind and feel the snow melt on my face. I hear the sounds of life around me. I am curious about what I experience and what might be far beyond. I am alive! Thank you for love and faithfulness that comes to me in the amazing environment you have made. Amen

God's open door

"So I say to you, Ask, and it will be given to you; search, and you will find; knock, and the door will be opened for you. For everyone who asks receives, and everyone who searches finds, and for everyone who knocks, the door will be opened." *Luke 11:9-10*

Jesus invites us into an active relationship with God. We are given permission to ask, search, and knock. We enter into a dynamic interaction with the Lord of Life.

It was after Jesus taught his disciples to pray the Lord's Prayer that he brought this teaching of openness to our relationship with God.

We must remember, the disciples were growing into a relationship with God as they were learning of God's purpose for them and for the world through Jesus. They were beginning to discover their own mission. The course they would be taking would require great personal sacrifice. And the truth is, they didn't yet have a clue how much sacrifice they would be making.

At first, it may seem to us that in this scripture about prayer, Jesus invites using God to grant our selfish desires. Ask for a million dollars and you get it. Ask for a Porsche and God will give you one! Don't we all wish this were true? (By the way, Ray misspelled the word *Porsche*. In his defense, he never had the money to buy one, so why would he be able to spell it correctly, right? Perfection isn't possible for any of us.)

The invitation to ask, search, and knock invites the follower of Jesus into a purposeful and open relationship with God. We ask for help in growing into a deeper relationship with God. We search for what is most important in making life meaningful. We knock and are promised that the door of God's redeeming purpose is open to us.

As you ask, search, and knock on the door of God's heart, may you find a deeper connection to God's love.

Forgive me when I live on the surface of life and think of you as a sugar daddy god who will give me whatever I want. Help me discover your love for me each day of my life. Amen

Letting light shine

"No one after lighting a lamp puts it in a cellar, but on the lampstand so that those who enter may see the light. Your eye is the lamp of your body. If your eye is healthy, your whole body is full of light; but if it is not healthy, your body is full of darkness. Therefore consider whether the light in you is not darkness. If then your whole body is full of light, with no part of it in darkness, it will be as full of light as when a lamp gives you light with its rays." *Luke 11:33-36*

A children's Sunday school song called "This Little Light of Mine" comes to mind as we read this text. Many of us learned from earliest days that we should let our light shine. We are to bring light to a dark world as we follow Christ.

Ray whimsically drew the lighthouse with a "light switch" mounted on it. Sometimes, I have joked, I wish I had a switch. When the alarm rings in the morning I wish a switch would turn on in my brain and wake me up. When I'm tired after a long day, I wish a switch could be turned on to give me more energy to finish work I need to complete. But this is idle fantasy.

The light imagined in this text is light that enlightens the whole person. A lighthouse shining in a treacherous sea reveals the shore and rocks that threaten the ships that sail by. When light shines in darkness it isn't always pretty. What it reveals may be difficult. The light gives us information and helps us make better decisions.

In the history of Western civilization before the time of the reformer Martin Luther, historians speak of the Dark Ages. Superstition, fear, magical thinking, and authoritarian rule prevailed. This was followed by a creative burst of freedom and knowledge in Europe. It became known as the Enlightenment. Martin Luther attempted and then succeeded to survive his challenge to reform the church. Intellectual freedom and nonconformity was tolerated. Europe would soon experience a renaissance. We have all benefited from the age of Enlightenment as new discoveries and advances in understanding of cosmology, science, and medicine would eventually lay the foundation of the modern world.

With this rapid change, has your spiritual enlightenment kept up with the enlightenment that makes possible the advances of knowledge around you? How can we keep from slipping back into an age of spiritual darkness fed by fear, superstition, magical thinking, and authoritarian rule?

Enlighten our hearts and minds that we can see more clearly the challenges that face us each day. Amen

God's gifts cannot be purchased

Now when Simon saw that the Spirit was given through the laying on of the apostles' hands, he offered them money, saying, "Give me also this power so that anyone on whom I lay my hands may receive the Holy Spirit." But Peter said to him, "May your silver perish with you, because you thought you could obtain God's gift with money! You have no part or share in this, for your heart is not right before God. Repent therefore of this wickedness of yours, and pray to the Lord that, if possible, the intent of your heart may be forgiven you. For I see that you are in the gall of bitterness and the chains of wickedness." Simon answered, "Pray for me to the Lord, that nothing of what you have said may happen to me." *Acts 8:18-24*

In our society it seems that everything gets reduced to money. Whatever is of value has a price. We measure the standard of living in a community or society based on money. The fascination with the stock market as a measure of how well the economy is doing illustrates how significant the role of money is—our investments and pensions depend on it. There is no doubt that money and money management are highly important in the worldwide economy.

The question is: Can economics fully account for what makes a society good, beneficial, and successful? Can everything that has value be bought?

We are tempted to view ourselves as measured by our financial success. If I make a lot of money I am more valuable than if I make less money. I may fancy myself as a self-made person who is in love with his or her creator. We may think "I did it all!" We also may view other people who are less financially successful as failures or a drag on society.

In the scripture story from Acts, when an observer, named Simon, saw how the Holy Spirit was given through the apostles by laying on of hands, he wanted that power, too. He was a successful person. Wouldn't it be great to have that kind of power? So he offered the apostles money and asked them to give him this power to make people receive the Holy Spirit! That would be a really great trick! Right? Wrong.

The condemnation of Simon was swift and strong. No one can buy the Holy Spirit. God's Spirit is priceless. In fact it is freely given as a gift of grace. Simon's heart was not right before God. He was in danger of condemnation because of reducing God to a price tag. There are some things that money can't buy.

Lord, help me see your gifts of grace and priceless Spirit in this money-obsessed world. Amen

Looking up

The heavens are telling the glory of God; and the firmament proclaims his handiwork. *Psalm 19:1*

In winter there is nothing so stunning as a cloudless night with the moon reflected on the snow. The cold, crisp air allows for clarity to see the planets and stars shining above. The length of darkness during the short days of winter allows more time for those of us in the northern climates to catch a glimpse of the majesty and depth of sky and space. It is amazing to behold!

Often on a clear night in January, the northern lights can be seen dancing and moving along the atmosphere providing a marvelous visual symphony. There is so much we can see if we look up more often!

Whether winter, spring, summer, or fall, "the heavens are telling the glory of God." If we live in urban areas where streetlights interfere with our view of the sky, it may be necessary to go to a place where the sky can be seen. There is nothing more life changing than to take time to look up and see what is above us. Whether we see clouds, airplanes, or satellites moving across our view—or stars that have continued to shine for millions and billions of years—when we look up we discover how much we don't see as we move about in our daily life.

When was the last time you sat and looked into an evening sky? How long has it been since you have gazed into the depths of sky and space? What do you remember from the last time you stopped to look and see what is around you?

Thank you, Lord, for giving me the capacity to see and wonder at majesty and mystery of all that you have made. Amen

Being old is difficult

Do not cast me off in the time of old age; do not forsake me when my strength is spent. Psalm 71:9

"When you get older you know more, but you forget most of it. What can I do? I just accept it. That's the kind of person I am" (someone suffering from early stage of Alzheimer's).

When we have had a long life of experiences we gain knowledge, awareness, perspective, and more. But sometimes it disappears because of diseases that affect one's brain function and memory. Nobody looks forward to that!

Listen to this man's account: "I'm going to be ninety-three next month. Nobody knows what it's like being old like this. Younger people don't understand. They haven't experienced it. I can't blame them; I'd have been the same way when I was younger. After you're ninety, people don't think you know anything. They treat you like you're a nobody. But I do know a lot! I am important. But nobody wants to hear it. Then I go to my bed and lie down. But that isn't the answer. I have to get up and keep walking. I can't just lie around. I have to keep moving or my legs will quit. I used to go out and walk to church by myself. I also used to walk up the street and then back. I am afraid to do that now because I get confused about where I am. I don't want to be out on the street and have someone realize I am confused and they would want to take advantage of me."

You have heard from two experts what it's like to be old with memory loss. It is difficult growing old when memory-robbing diseases threaten us. Would that we could all grow old with complete memories and wonderful health!

When we are small children, being a teenager seems old. And as Ray Johnson's cartoon suggests it is "really rough" going without hat and boots in winter! Remember those days? Much more waits the young as they grow through their early years into adulthood and throughout the life-span to old age.

Have you faced difficulties of health, fortune, relationships, or despair in your life? How have you faced these challenges? How are you facing those challenges today?

Lord, forget me not when I am sick, poor, shunned, forgotten, and old. I rely daily upon your mercy and grace for all my life challenges. Amen

God's power in nature

The animals take cover; they remain in their dens. The tempest comes out from its chamber, the cold from the driving winds. The breath of God produces ice, and the broad waters become frozen. He loads the clouds with moisture; he scatters his lightning through them. At his direction they swirl around over the face of the whole earth to do whatever he commands them. He brings the clouds to punish [people], or to water his earth and show his love. Job 37:8-13 NIV (Elihu describes God's power in nature to Job)

Those of us in northern climates are accused of obsessing over the weather. Probably it is because the changes in weather have an important effect on us. The weather is always changing. Extreme cold or extreme storms are common. Nothing gets one's blood flowing better than a serious stretch of cold weather or a major blizzard. Ray's cartoon about how to read a Minnesota thermometer gives clever ways to "spin" the bad news of a really cold temperature.

Severe weather is also dangerous. An elderly man told me about his uncle who froze to death many years ago out in the cold of a blizzard. It's hard to forget a tragedy like that.

Elihu, a friend to Job, claimed that God's power can be seen in nature and the storms, ice, lightening, and cold that threaten life. At such times even the animals take cover and remain in their dens. This scripture, no doubt, lays down the belief that lies behind the practice of insurance companies to refer to natural disasters as "acts of God."

What do you think about the belief that bad weather and storms are acts of God to punish us? As Elihu puts it, "He brings the clouds to punish people." On the other hand do you believe that God brings rain to the earth to "show his love" as Elihu claims? Or does weather such as storms and life-threatening cold happen without regard to our moral behavior or faithfulness to God? What is your belief about the power of God in nature?

Help me discern the truth regarding what God's purpose is the midst of severe weather and winter storms. Amen

Telling the truth

[Jesus said,] "But because I tell the truth, you do not believe me. Which of you convicts me of sin? If I tell the truth, why do you not believe me? Whoever is from God hears the words of God. The reason you do not hear them is that you are not from God." The Jews answered him, "Are we not right in saying that you are a Samaritan and have a demon?" Jesus answered, "I do not have a demon; but I honor my Father, and you dishonor me." *John 8:45-49*

In this scripture reading Jesus was trying to tell the truth to his detractors. It was hard. They didn't believe him. In fact, they accused him of having a demon. They called him names, including labeling him a Samaritan. It was a conversation that eventually ended with a threat of violence. They picked up stones to stone him. But Jesus was able to sneak away. The conversation ended badly. His truth was not welcomed among those questioning him.

Have you experienced such difficult conversations? Was there some truth that needed telling that you knew would bring a reaction?

In your church or community have you had difficult conversations that needed truth telling that no one wanted to hear? How did those conversations end?

What is the cost of hiding the truth, avoiding issues? Many don't like arguments, even regarding such talk as "un-Christian." On the other hand, some seek controversy and like the game of arguing about "who's right?" and take pleasure in such banter.

What is the purpose of "telling the truth"? How do you know when you or another is speaking the truth? Can we have a meaningful relationship with another without honesty about one's identity, needs, and dreams? What have been your experiences with telling someone your truth?

O Lord, you know what's in my heart. Sometimes I don't know what I think or believe. Sometimes I'm afraid to tell the truth because others may reject me. Help me tell the truth about my desires, my feelings, my concerns, my needs, my fears, and my dreams. Without truth, I feel empty and like a deceiver. To tell you the truth, it's hard to tell you the truth. Have mercy, O Lord. Have mercy upon me. Amen

An extreme makeover

But you, O Lord, reign forever; your throne endures to all generations.
Why have you forgotten us completely? Why have you forsaken us these
many days? Restore us to yourself, O Lord, that we may be restored; renew
our days as of old— *Lamentations 5:19-21*

After years of life experiences that are challenging and sometimes difficult, we may feel
worn down and in a rut. Our enthusiasm for life is gone, and we live in a routine that seems
pointless and even lifeless. Jeremiah's lament expresses such a feeling when he says, "Why
have you forgotten us completely? Why have you forsaken us these many days?" An economic
crash, a loss of a job, a mortgage upside down, an uncertain future with health problems,
and difficult family dynamics. Who hasn't had such moments? Is this all there is to life?

A reality TV show you may remember called *Extreme Makeover* grabbed the attention of
many viewers. We were told stories about a family who faced insurmountable challenges of
poverty and was struggling without hope as they scratched together what little they could
manage in order to live from day to day.

Enter the Extreme Makeover leader and his or her team. They came with great fanfare,
many resources, and much drama as they proclaimed that this family would receive an
extreme makeover. The family was usually whisked away to a vacation spot of enjoyment.
Meanwhile, in a few days their home was demolished and a new one built and finished with
everything the family could ever dream of. At the end the family returned and the emotion
of seeing what was made new grabbed one's heartstrings. If only we all could experience
an extreme makeover!

We all wish for renewal and restoration, a return to living life fully and with purpose. At
certain times in our lives we may try to start over, make a move, try something different, or
reconnect with something we've longed for. Have you had such a time in your life? Are you
at a point where you need that extreme makeover to lift your spirits? If so, you are not alone.

Restore us to yourself, O Lord, that we may be restored; renew our days as of old. Amen

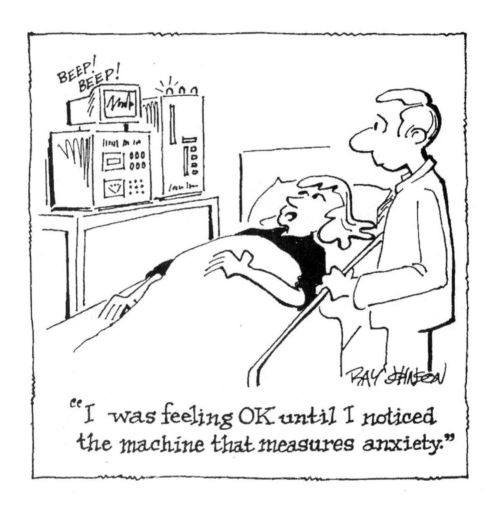

Anxiety

Cast all your anxiety on him, because he cares for you. 1 Peter 5:7

We live in an age of anxiety. Some of us are more exposed to anxiety than others. When we were children some of us were anxious about doing well in school, passing a test, making a grade, being accepted by friends. Others seemed not to worry. Learning and socializing came easy.

As adults many of us learned about the uncertainties of the economy, the weather, the expectations of work, and the challenges of living with or working with difficult people.

As we grow older we may become anxious about the well-being of our children and grandchildren. And of course, we can worry about our health. One man said to me, "I gave up going to organ recitals. All my old friends do is talk about their organs—kidneys, bowels, heart, and liver."

What anxieties plague you in the course of your daily life?

In Ray's cartoon, the medical technology triggers anxiety in the patient. The visiting pastor sees the worry and appears, himself, focused upon the machines, not the one he is visiting. Has that happened to you?

When you, as pastor, lay minister, or friend of someone sick and anxious, what do you say when you visit? How are you present to the person you've come to see? When a person is anxious, what does he or she need?

When I was a young pastor, I was asked to visit an elderly woman in the hospital who was just diagnosed with a very serious illness that was untreatable. I remember that I was the one experiencing anxiety when I went to visit. As we talked I was avoiding the subject for why I had come, not knowing how to bring up the obvious subject of her terminal illness. This elderly woman who was very pale and thin recognized my anxious condition. She smiled, and said, "Pastor, in case you are wondering, I'm going to be okay." I laugh, now, when I remember her.

Sometimes the sick comfort us in our anxieties. We all have times when we need reassurance. It's important to name our anxieties and to address the deeper needs that we have for love, forgiveness, acceptance, and connection.

The following Bible verse hung on the wall in our dining room when I was a child: "Cast all your anxiety on him, because he cares for you" (1 Peter 5:7). My mother suffered from anxiety. She needed to be reminded of what this scripture said. And so do I. Do you?

Managing resources

Through sloth the roof sinks in, and through indolence the house leaks.
Feasts are made for laughter; wine gladdens life, and money meets every
need. *Ecclesiastes 10:18-19*

The words from Ecclesiastes are an example of truths recorded and preserved from antiquity.
The scripture verses may not be ones you memorized in Sunday school. But when you read
them, you probably recognize their message.

In our church life and in our personal life we are responsible to manage our resources
for living and for mission. You may identify with Ray's cartoon showing money falling out
of his pocket as he walks along. "Where, oh where has all of the money gone?" we may
wonder as we look at our bank account at the end of the month. Money just seems to fly
out of our pockets. We all are conditioned to be consumers. Advertising messages tempt
us hundreds of times a day to spend money. But what if the money flies out of our pockets
and we forget our basic needs?

Driving home one night I pushed the button to open the garage door as I had done
thousands of time before. This time I heard a loud grinding sound as the door stalled
half open. Then I heard a loud BAM! The door shuddered and slammed shut. The tension
spring for the garage door had broken. I was stunned and surprised! I had not planned for
this to happen. Have you ever experienced an unwelcome and expensive surprise? What
happened? How did it affect you?

So what happens if the roof sinks in and water leaks into your house or your church as
Ecclesiastes mentions? What effect do such events have on your sense of safety, well-being,
and mission as a family and as a church?

Times for feasting and laughter are also needed in life. We cherish celebrations of
weddings, baptisms, special dinners, and fellowship in our lives and in our churches. And
money can meet needs when it is given purpose. Budgets help give purpose to our money
in church and home. With that purpose we can be good stewards.

*Lord, give us courage to face the challenges of being good stewards. Give us wisdom to
prepare for the unexpected and to help each other when the unexpected comes. Amen*

GLOBAL ECONOMY...

RAY JOHNSON

Stewardship of the earth

Then God said, "Let us make humankind in our image, according to our likeness; and let them have dominion over the fish of the sea, and over the birds of the air, and over the cattle, and over all the wild animals of the earth, and over every creeping thing that creeps upon the earth." *Genesis 1:26*

The familiar story of creation places human beings in charge of the earth. Domination, control, authority, and power are all words that come to mind when reading these creation texts and hear we are created in the likeness of God.

In our lifetime, humans have really fulfilled the role of domination. At nearly seven billion strong and growing, humans have touched nearly every part of the earth and affected the life of all living creatures wherever we live. With a responsibility for all the fish, birds, cattle, wild animals, and creeping things, one would hope that we are good stewards. What is your sense of how we humans are doing in fulfilling the responsibility we have been given over all living creatures? What good things are we doing? What negative impacts are we creating and what problems we are facing?

Ray's cartoon pictures a crude pipe that circles the earth and converts everything into money. We call it the global economy. It seems that we convert most everything into a commodity so that it can be priced and pumped around the globe. When everything is valued in terms of money, what effect does this have on life on this planet?

We humans really are god-like in our relationship to all of life on the earth where we live. We rearrange forests, open prairies and mountainsides to be filled with urban and suburban homes and businesses. Cars, trains, airlines all provide easy travel anywhere we wish to go. In the last seventy years humans for the first time understand the language of all life. We can modify plants so that they grow with higher yields. One person can run a machine to sow or cultivate large fields within a few hours of time. Only a century ago great numbers of farmers with horses and simple tools would work weeks to do what one farmer can do today. What changes have you seen in technology in your lifetime?

Because of our human activity, the earth today has been changed in many ways from what it was 100 years ago. We do dominate the earth today. In many ways we seem to believe that we can do anything that pleases us in our exercise of power and freedom without bad result. Such a belief is dangerous.

What challenges and responsibilities do you see that we have today as stewards of the earth?

Lord, help us overcome our wrongdoing and disregard for your creation. Amen

Heading toward disaster

The wise are cautious and turn away from evil, but the fool throws off restraint and is careless. *Proverbs 14:16*

Have you ever lived dangerously? Even once? I laugh every time I see this cartoon. I can imagine the skier thinking, "Oh, this isn't going to turn out well!" How would you imagine the story ending for the skier as he heads into the midcourse correction?

Risk taking is everywhere. In the fast-paced society we have created there are many stories of risky behavior and associated disasters. A risk-taking skier triggers a snow avalanche killing many, including himself. A train hauling oil cars derails and many oil tankers explode. A speeding car loses control on the interstate and crashes during rush hour causing a massive pile up of cars and trucks and people are injured and die. We hear stories like this every day.

I've sensed a trend in our globalized world toward a faster pace of change. A new communication technology is introduced and becomes obsolete almost immediately. There is faster internet, faster images on our television, faster food service, faster banking—everything faster, faster, faster. When we are moving, consuming, communicating at increasing speed, what happens if we are confronted by need of a midcourse correction in our lifestyle? Is the increasing speed of technology development a symptom of high-risk behavior? Or is it a necessary and mostly a good part of modern life that we need to adopt?

Do our fast-paced lifestyles need any words of caution? What if we crash upon impact when we lose our high-flying job and income? Or what might happen to our rapid consumption when we face product and food shortages due to droughts, monster storms, or other natural disasters? Will the fast pace of living give us momentum that we can use to negotiate difficult changes we may face? I'm full of questions; what are your thoughts?

I propose that we are all like the skier. We are thrilled as we career down the slope of life, but we see trouble straight ahead. Now what do we do? According to the collected wisdom of Proverbs 14:16, "the wise are cautious . . . but the fool throws off restraint . . ." We can test this wisdom because we have the rest of our lifetime to attempt to negotiate the midcourse corrections we will need to make.

Lord, give us courage to face the days ahead with confidence we can successfully negotiate the midcourse corrections needed in our journey of life. Amen

Loss of economic status

For the needy shall not always be forgotten, nor the hope of the poor perish forever. *Psalm 9:18*

I've worked as a chaplain for more than twenty years at a very special place called Ebenezer Care Center in Minneapolis, Minnesota. Its mission began in 1917 during WWI as a home for the homeless Norwegian immigrants who were too old to work and had no family or money. They came to their pastors and churches not knowing what to do.

Six Norwegian Lutheran church denominations set aside their theological differences and worked together to create a place to live for those who were aged and poor. It really was a poor house for immigrants of Norwegian language, culture, and religion. At an annual meeting a few years into the mission, the leader of Ebenezer reflected upon the situation by saying, "Not even the heathen treat their poor as badly as we!" His language reflected the times in which he lived. And it reminded me that Christians still fail to care about others in need right in their own community. It is also worth noting that in 1917 and into the years of the Great Depression, most people supporting "the poor at Ebenezer" were struggling financially themselves.

My dear friend Ray who drew the cartoons in this book knew something about living on the edge financially. With debilitating symptoms of depression that haunted him for years, he found himself struggling with limited resources. "I've lost touch with my inner wallet" would be his way of naming the spiritual experience of being poor. For a time in his ministry he worked at Augustana Lutheran Church's Crossroads program in south Minneapolis, Minnesota. One night as he was dishing up soup in the kitchen for the homeless he looked up and saw one of his adopted sons he had not seen for a long time standing in the soup line. His life, too, was a struggle.

It is common that when we have experienced a struggle we better understand others going through similar experiences. People who have lost jobs and homes can relate to others in the same situation. People with cancer band together to support each other. Ray and I both lived with the symptoms of depression. One day we made a pact that we be bonded as brothers to each other. In that way we were never alone in our days struggling with despair. That commitment was life giving for both of us.

In our church communities, can we make commitments to be brothers and sisters to each other for support in daily life? Can we form extended families in deeper ways? We never know what tomorrow brings. Strong friendships can help see us through whatever may come. Belonging to a community of faith that is nonjudgmental is priceless. And being loved and accepted by God and another human being is redemptive.

Lord, you promise that the needy shall not always be forgotten, nor the hope of the poor perish forever. May it be so for all of us. Amen

May I raise a question?

Then certain individuals came down from Judea and were teaching the brothers, "Unless you are circumcised according to the custom of Moses, you cannot be saved." And after Paul and Barnabas had no small dissension and debate with them, Paul and Barnabas and some of the others were appointed to go up to Jerusalem to discuss this question with the apostles and the elders. *Acts 15:1-2*

Questions have been part of the Christian experience from the very beginning. We see that in the text from Acts 15. The question was raised about whether it was necessary to be circumcised according to the custom of Moses in order to be saved. The debate was taken by Paul and Barnabas to Jerusalem for further discussion. The question was important and needed an answer. There is a long tradition of religious controversy over theology, teachings, and practices in the church. Some questions have led to conflict and religious wars. So raising questions can be dangerous.

Just ask Martin Luther about danger after he posted his ninety-five theses on the church door at Wittenberg, Germany, to raise questions about religious practices of his day. Because of his questioning, he was asked to recant his writings. Luther refused. Eventually Luther was excommunicated by the Catholic Church and was under threat of death. Or you can ask Fredrik O. Nilsson about danger when he questioned the beliefs and practices of the Lutheran Church in Sweden and illegally established the first Baptist church there. As a result, he was arrested, convicted of heresy in a court of law by the Lutheran Church of Sweden, and banished from the country in 1850. In 1854 he brought a band of twenty-one Swedish followers to America in search of religious freedom. Three of them were my ancestors. Later on in life Nilsson continued to question. He questioned the inspiration of the Bible and the deity of Christ to the dismay of his Baptist converts.

Living in America gives every person the right to believe and think as they wish. Every religious group is granted the right to freely assemble and worship in whatever manner they choose. No police or religious authorities can arrest you for wrongly practicing your religious worship and beliefs.

In religion as in life, questions can have powerful consequences. During your lifetime have questions been raised in your local church or denomination that created controversy? What was the question and what happened? What questions do you still live with and wonder about? Have you ever been afraid to ask questions for fear of disapproval or harmful consequences?

Lord, give us courage to explore the questions that trouble us. Amen

Childish behavior disorder

When I was a child, I spoke like a child, I thought like a child, I reasoned like a child; when I became an adult, I put an end to childish ways.
1 Corinthians 13:11

If you have children or grandchildren, you are familiar with what Ray called "childish behavior disorder." Of course, most of us are wise enough to know that what his cartoon illustrates is simply children acting like children. Running, jumping, playing, acting "goofy," and laughing is what I see in children as they explore their world and relationships.

Do you remember the days in your life of being a child? My mother who didn't like a lot of running and jumping would say, "If you want to play go outside. Don't jump around on the furniture in the house!" So I spent a lot of time outside.

A nurse with whom I worked for many years told stories about her young boys playing hockey (with their hockey sticks) in the dining room when she wasn't looking. Every family has stories like this. What stories do you have from your family?

As children we are often impulsive, carefree, looking for fun, and wanting excitement. And sometimes we are careless. One summer night I remember playing outside with my cousins at grandma's farmhouse. We were running in the dark around the house as fast as we could. Suddenly my feet left the ground as my neck hit a clothesline, and I fell flat on my back on the ground. Needless to say, that was no longer fun. But it was a lesson in life. Bad things can happen when you are not careful. My childish ways were tempered just a little bit.

Being a child is essential in order to develop into a mature human being. And when responsibilities become important and we face difficulties and challenges, we grow up. But I have noticed as a grandfather of twenty grandchildren that it is still fun to play with children and slip back into "childish behavior disorder." So have a little fun, but don't hook your neck on a clothesline!

High-risk behaviors

And everyone who hears these words of mine and does not act on them will
be like a foolish man who built his house on sand. *Matthew 7:26*

High-risk behaviors can include many things. Ray's cartoon give a sense that the man in the
bucket tackling a job on electric lines may be a guy in the wrong job. He may underestimate
the dangers he faces and risk injury, even death. There are many stories about people who
suffer serious injury in their work and life.

In the first parish I served in the 1970s, the husband of one of my volunteer secretaries
was a man who worked for the Rural Electric Association as a lineman. One day he took a
direct shock of electricity while working on an electric line attached to a pole on which he
had climbed for repairs. The charge caused him to fall off the pole and onto the ground.
He had burns from the electric charge on his neck as it traveled into and out of his body.
Somehow when he fell and hit the ground, the jar may have restarted his heart—and he lived
to tell about it. Ever after he lived with permanent injury. You may know of those who suffer
from injury due to high-risk dangers or freak accidents that can occur on many worksites.

The story Jesus tells about the foolish man who built his house on sand illustrates a
spiritual truth as well as a moral lesson about those who ignore risks and build their homes
in dangerous places needlessly risking their lives and future. Matthew 7 is a section of Jesus'
teachings. The chapter ends with the parable of the wise and foolish builders. Those who
are foolish disregard his teachings and warnings. But those who pay attention and learn
will be like the man who built his house on the rock.

Have you ever tried doing a job you weren't prepared for? Many of us who are amateurs
know about this. Reading instructions or watching a YouTube training video might help.
Then again, it might be the better wisdom to know when you are in the wrong job and need
help from someone who knows what to do. Still, it is tempting to take risks.

Seeing where people live today, I wonder why do so many people still build their homes
on sand along sea and ocean? Why do so many who build homes ignore risks of nature like
avalanches, super storms, and hurricanes? How long can we ignore rising oceans and melting
glaciers? Why do we deny and ignore such risks? Where is our wisdom and common sense?

As we assess life decisions, teach us to be wise and avoid what is foolish. Amen

Learning curves

While [Paul] was making this defense [to King Agrippa], Festus [Governor of Caesarea] exclaimed, "You are out of your mind, Paul! Too much learning is driving you insane!" But Paul said, "I am not out of my mind, most excellent Festus, but I am speaking the sober truth." *Acts 26:24-25*

The story of Paul's defense, which was more like a witness before King Agrippa, is one of the greatest speeches recorded in scripture. When Governor of Caesarea, Porcius Festus, heard the cogent, complex, and highly learned presentation by Paul, he lost it and blurted out, "You are out of your mind, Paul!"

But Paul wasn't buying it. He was doing just fine. It was Governor Festus who was losing it. Festus wasn't sure where Paul was going with his speech and was afraid his appearance before King Agrippa would turn out badly. He truly thought Paul may have spent too much time alone in prison studying scripture and reasoned the isolation and obsessive reading probably had driven him insane. Paul dismissed this assertion. When Paul's verdict was finally given by the court, he was cleared of the charges against him. Then "Agrippa said to Festus, 'This man could have been set free if he had not appealed to the emperor'" (Acts 26:32). True. But the stage was now set for Paul to actually make witness to the gospel before Caesar himself. The learning curve regarding Paul's mission was on course. The bigger picture came into view and events would take Paul to the very seat of Roman power.

The words of Festus remind me of Ray's cartoon of the learning curve. I look at the image and laugh. I'm the guy flying over the edge! Trying to understand everything at once is too much! Maybe it's true that too much learning can drive someone crazy.

Learning curves can come in many shapes depending upon what one needs to learn. Knowledge and experience are measured by how fast one can absorb new knowledge and apply it through experience. Every student experiences the process. How do we keep up with new information? Can we adapt, change, readjust to what is changing, and absorb the new knowledge about what is coming next? Some of us land off the road and in the ditch when the learning curve becomes too sharp. But fortunately, we usually can shake off the dust and re-engage in the challenges.

What challenges you? What new information have you gained and applied in your daily life? How is your purpose in life engaged in learning? Are you able to laugh when something doesn't make sense?

Lord, encourage us to achieve understanding as we apply new knowledge into our life experiences and purpose. Amen

Mental weather forecast

Satisfy us in the morning with your steadfast love, so that we may rejoice and be glad all our days. Make us glad as many days as you have afflicted us, and as many years as we have seen evil. Let your work be manifest to your servants, and your glorious power to their children. *Psalm 90:14-16*

Ray's struggle with depression was evident in his cartoons. Here the television news mental health weather forecaster is bringing a hopeful forecast showing the cloudy blues and the depression front being pushed away by the bright sunshine of serenity. Finding serenity in daily life is a great hope.

The psalmist's words reflect a similar hope seeking God's love to come and bless our days, hoping we will be glad for as many days and years as we have seen evil, despair, and sadness. The psalmist also asks that steadfast love be made manifest to the children, the next generation of God's servants, which gives us hope.

I caution thinking that a positive attitude can be willed into existence to cure chronic depression. Such a prescription for happiness is often received by the person who is suffering depression with more despair and a deepening of emotional isolation. Unfortunately, risk of suicide is common when people perceive they are helpless and stuck in a gloomy fog where there is no way out.

The mental health weather forecast will be much brighter if the problem is addressed with effective medical and mental health treatment. A person suffering depression often feels shame, inadequacy, and unworthiness that may lead to avoiding treatment. It is important to understand that the shame and other feelings of deprivation are powerful. They must be addressed and acknowledged with gentle grace and serenity. This takes time and patience. And sometimes the gloom prevails and refuses to go away. Ray is one who had to live with the gloom for years. It never quit hanging around. So he embraced it and used it to understand others who suffered. That's what he did for me.

The spirituality of the Twelve Steps of Alcoholics Anonymous, Narcotics Anonymous, or Co-Dependents Anonymous are disciplines that may be helpful for someone coping with a case of deep hopelessness and despair. Underlying addiction is often a mood problem. It is beneficial down the road in recovery to find support to repair and build important and intimate relationships as one lives with the changing mental weather in one's brain.

So, how's your mental health weather forecast looking in your brain and mind today? What kind of weather map might you draw to communicate what's going on inside of you? Pay attention to your mental and spiritual weather conditions each day. Seek help if you see a bad day coming.

Lord, grant me the serenity to accept the things I cannot change, the courage to change the things I can, and the wisdom to know the difference. Amen (Serenity Prayer attributed to Reinhold Niebuhr)

Harshness and softness

A soft answer turns away wrath, but a harsh word stirs up anger. Proverbs 15:1

This cartoon by Ray uses animals to portray something about how we perceive others and how they perceive us.

My father remembered going to a summer Swedish Lutheran Bible camp as a youngster in the 1930s in South Dakota. He said, "The pastors were dressed in their black suits and clericals. They would sit under the trees with scowls on their face watching us kids making sure we didn't have any fun." His experience was memorable because of the intimidation he experienced as a youngster by those who were pastors of his day.

Appearances are powerful in shaping opinion. Perceptions can create a sense of emotional distance and distrust. Or someone's appearance can draw us in. I have noticed that when a baby comes into the room, we are all drawn together. Why? Isn't it the appearance of innocence, softness, and cuteness? We feel connected emotionally to the baby and to each other as well. Whether little children, a bunny rabbit, a kitten, or puppy—they can bring out our soft side.

The first impression I had of a physician I met one day was that of a grouch. His face was stern, no gleam in his eye, nor any hint of pleasure. I didn't know if I wanted to know him. Sometime later I was invited to a party to celebrate a friend's milestone birthday. The grouchy physician was there. Was I surprised! Underneath his grouchy face was a funny sense of humor and a soft side I hadn't seen nor expected.

How do others perceive you when you when they first meet you? Have you ever asked or wondered? What first impression have you had of someone you met only later to discover you were mistaken?

Lord, you made all of us capable of having a soft side that attracts and nourishes. Even those of us with a crusty exterior have a soft spot inside. With your grace continue to soften our hearts. Amen

Remember the days of old

Remember the days of old, consider the years long past; ask your father, and he will inform you; your elders, and they will tell you. *Deuteronomy 32:7*

In recent decades more attention has been given to ancestry, recording memories and family history. Ancestors in my family emigrated from Scandinavia to the United States in the decades between 1854 and the 1880s. For those immigrants, remembering the days of old was painful. Many didn't want to talk about the "old country." They were now Americans; this was a new land and a new place of opportunity. So they created the foundation for community with churches, schools, businesses, farms, and raising their families. But little was shared with the children and grandchildren about memories of old, especially of the old country.

In the early 1970s a new invention called the audiocassette tape recorder was marketed. I bought one and went to a nursing home where an elderly woman whom I knew lived. She was the only living cousin to one of my grandmothers who had died when I was three years old. I knew little about that part of the family. I asked her if I could record her as she told me memories about the days of her childhood and what she knew about when her parents immigrated to America and South Dakota. I still have that audiotape with her voice and the memories she shared that day now long ago.

Our society is obsessed with rapid change and anxiously focused on the future. Many, especially the young, don't know from where they came. Whether family or church, we need to consider the years long past. A family reunion or a church anniversary is a great opportunity to gather stories and interview elders.

Have you captured the stories of founding members or children of founding families of the church? These stories need to be remembered so we know and remember from where we came. Have you dug into the memory mine of elders in your family to record their history? What stories have you found worth retelling? What memories and stories were you told that have helped you understand your family and church and what they believe, celebrate, and value?

And whatever your age, practice digging into your own memory to understand what events and experiences are shaping you and your purpose in life. As Ray's cartoon announces, "Memory Mine. It's all in here someplace."

Lord, bless us with memories told to us from of old. As we reflect upon our history, help us see your guiding hand and grace that sustains us and leads us. Then we, too, can tell the next generations rising before us from where they have come. Amen

Confessing sins

Therefore confess your sins to one another, and pray for one another, so that you may be healed. The prayer of the righteous is powerful and effective. *James 5:16*

Ray's humor regarding confessing sin and failures touches the shame we have when thinking of our wrongs.

Many of us were raised with the idea that we are to avoid failure, not screw up, get As in school, and find a good job after college or grad school. And it wouldn't hurt if we joined a church or some club to secure our social network and place in community.

Climbing the ladder of respectability and success can be rewarding. It can also keep us so busy that we don't notice the little things we are missing along the way. And the little things can pile up and surprise us.

In the middle of life we may have an awakening to the unfortunate decisions we made. We have experienced something that reminds us that decisions or lack of decisions have consequences. We might look back with regrets for not taking an opportunity or risk. On the other hand we might also regret having taken such a risk. Life is full of opportunities and also risks.

Ray's cartoon is full of comparisons, shameful comparisons. As a failure, did you screw things up better than your former friends, he asks. Of course, there is the humor of seeing in ourselves something that we mostly keep hidden.

So what kind of a list might you write? Would it be a humorous one? Or might it be a painful one? Actually, a humorous list is really a list that lets you laugh at your pain. And that is the point of all of this. Can we keep perspective on our perceived failures? Or do our perceived failures threaten to crush us?

I hope you have some fun with this. And when you uncover something deeply hidden because of pain, it is worthwhile examining. Does it involve injury to another person? Are there amends to make? Is it a perceived failure you wrapped in shame and hid?

Maybe it's time to get out into sunlight and put some perspective, some humor, and some awareness on a past hurtful event. The purpose of admitting one's sins is so that you may be healed. It is not to be humiliated in public before a body of people who are strangers. Rather it is to be welcomed, embraced, and forgiven. Now wouldn't that be something if you could experience this healing in family, among friends and even in a community of faith?

Money talks

For the love of money is a root of all kinds of evil, and in their eagerness to be rich some have wandered away from the faith and pierced themselves with many pains. *1 Timothy 6:10*

We all have a relationship with money. We depend on it for daily transactions to buy and sell. Money is a means, not an end in itself. In fact, money is more symbolic than it is physically real.

Today what we call money is mostly an electronic entry in a computer somewhere recorded by a bank or business. Physical money in your pocket is almost a rarity.

We have learned recently the US Supreme Court determined that for political purposes, money is speech. Presumably the more money you have the more speech you can have. Thus if you have little or no money in our society, then, the logic is, you probably have very little speech. Money talks. Money buys what you desire. Money buys trips. Money buys influence. Money buys friendship. Money buys loyalty. Money saved buys security in later years. Just think of the security, affluence, and influence money promises!

In the first letter to Timothy, the wise elder, the apostle Paul observes how the eagerness to be rich has led many astray, away from faith and into much suffering. It is not money itself, which is a tool for transactions for goods and services that is a moral problem. But it is the *love* of money that is dangerous. Have you ever had a dangerous relationship with money?

In many families, money is considered a private matter. We can talk about our most intimate relationships in public, but money is still taboo. What is it that causes so many of us to be uncomfortable about our financial lives?

How would you describe your relationship with money? Does your money talk to you? What message does money speak to you when you look in your bank account or receive your monthly check? I'll leave it to you. You can decide whether or not to tell someone about this very personal and intimate relationship you have with money. Or you can talk about a safer subject like how well Viagra is working for you in the bedroom. I hope you laughed. That was a joke!

Watching bugs

But among the winged insects that walk on all fours you may eat those that have jointed legs above their feet, with which to leap on the ground. Of them you may eat: the locust according to its kind, the bald locust according to its kind, the cricket according to its kind, and the grasshopper according to its kind. Leviticus 11:21-22

Children are often fascinated by insects that scurry around. Watching bugs can be a wonderful summertime experience. Watch how the ants organize themselves dragging something large from one place to the other! See how far a grasshopper can jump!

Scripture does not offer much to encourage our fascination with bugs. Nearly every scripture verse says that insects are detestable and unclean so should not be eaten as food.

But in Leviticus there is an exception. Insects with jointed legs above their feet that leap on the ground are okay to eat. Anybody for chocolate-covered grasshoppers?

Those of us who are older may remember stories of swarms of grasshoppers and locust that ate every living thing. They even ate paint off houses during the dust storms of the 1930s in mid-America. Watching the bugs coming in swarms was fascinating but also terrifying. This experience created a strong fear of bugs that still lingers in our society.

Today we spray crops with chemicals to kill insects. We hire pest control professionals to protect our homes from the invasion of ants and termites. We douse our bodies with insect repellant in summer to avoid mosquito bites. It's clear that we humans hate certain insects we perceive may harm us and our crops. Yet it may be that those insects we hate are also food for birds that we love.

Ladybugs are welcome in our gardens. Do you know of bugs that are beneficial from our human point of view? As the world population grows to more than nine billion, the United Nations has recommended eating insects to address world hunger. According to the report, certain types of beetles, ants, crickets, and grasshoppers are good for you. It states, "Insects are healthy, nutritious alternatives to mainstream staples such as chicken, pork, beef and even fish (from ocean catch). . . . It is estimated that insects form part of the traditional diets of at least two billion people. More than 1,900 species have reportedly been used as food" ("Edible Insects; Future Prospects for Food and Feed Security," 2013).

Did I hear you say "yuck"? Most insects listed above were allowed to be eaten under the strict religious dietary rules of ancient Israel. Remember John the Baptist living on locusts and wild honey when in the wilderness proclaiming a call to repentance? Maybe it's time to take another look at bugs. Do you think God likes to watch bugs as much as children do? Maybe we all could take another look at bugs. Or is that too disgusting? I'm wondering if at the next church potluck dinner someone will bring a dish of crispy cricket snacks along with stir-fried locust dipped in wild honey?

"I suggest we put this incident behind us by not mentioning it again—except in the parking lot, on the phone, and in hushed, muffled tones over coffee cups."

Church controversies

A gossip goes about telling secrets, but one who is trustworthy in spirit keeps a confidence. Proverbs 11:13

Human nature hasn't changed much. Gossip is a universal activity as people share their opinions about others and circumstances that affect relationships.

Ray Johnson had a way of using his cartoons to say out loud what everyone is thinking. It's good to laugh when someone says out loud what we dare not admit.

Do you recall a time in your family or in your church when the rumor mill was activated by somebody's controversial action, belief, or behavior? How did the controversy arise? What role did gossip play in the larger family or community? Do you recall any consequences? Any reputations damaged? Any misunderstandings? Any behaviors that added pain and confusion to an already hurtful situation? Did people come to acceptance and reconciliation after the controversy? Did some leave the church community, or even the family, with hurt or anger?

How do we engage controversy in our church? Is it something we avoid? Do we seek out controversy in order to discuss some unmet needs being neglected? Do we quote the Bible and assert the authority of the pastor and council to stamp out a controversy? Like Ray Johnson's cartoon, do we suggest putting the incident behind us by not mentioning it again (except in the parking lot, on the phone, and so forth)?

I remember decades ago in public school taking debate. A subject was chosen and each participant was asked to argue for a certain side of the controversy. This usually involved drawing a slip of paper on which you were told what position you had to take in the debate. I was given opportunity to learn various sides to an issue and then given the opportunity to present a convincing argument when called upon. It was a skill that helped develop a person's ability to participate in our democracy. It was important that everyone had a right, and some skill, to express their views and opinions in the public discourse. The skill of debate was taught in the belief that we all had a constitutional right to have freedom of speech.

In your church, is freedom of speech exercised by anyone besides the pastor who preaches? Are differences of opinions allowed among members regarding religious and social matters or must everyone believe and think in a similar way in order to belong?

A major characteristic of conflict in churches is the notion that one belief is right and of God and another view point is wrong and of Satan. Sometimes pastors use this reasoning to maintain their authority. Other times, parishioners may disagree with the pastor and even call the pastor a heretic, like some of my ancestors did one Sunday during worship in their Baptist church. After contradicting the pastor in the midst of his sermon condemning him for wrong teaching, they dramatically marched out in front of all people gathered and left their church for good.

Can we live and worship together with differences of belief and opinion? In the midst of controversy great or small, where is God?

The fog of depression

"The way things are going these days, if you aren't depressed, there's something wrong with you."

I smiled when I heard those words—they were spoken by a friend over coffee. The reason I wanted to reconnect with him was because I had just been released from the hospital for treatment of depression. I was looking for reconnection and support, two very powerful nonpharmaceutical antidepressants.

As I was telling him of my recent experience and the diagnosis of major depression, he leaned back and said those famous words, "The way things are going these days, if you aren't depressed, there's something wrong with you." I laughed. Certainly there was an irony in his observation. We may be living sometimes in a culture of depression. Is feeling depressed a normative condition? Is walking around with your head in a fog something normal? It is a good practice to observe the influences and messages that may lead to feeling hopeless.

Further along in my time of recovery, I reconnected with Ray Johnson whose cartoons I am sharing with you. He also had faced the fog of depression. And in our common experience and need for understanding and support, we made a commitment to bond together as brothers. We had known each other from early days of seminary education. We traveled in similar circles as pastors in the Lutheran church during our early years. But now we were in the middle of life and each of us had faced the darkness and fog of depression.

The cartoon I chose for this reflection helps me laugh at the unhappy condition of depression. As Ray would do, he drew a cartoon as a way to cope. My mind is a fog (says he) but your nose is clear (says she)! As we all know, having a clear mind with plugged sinuses can also make for a bad day. We all need perspective in order to laugh.

The Centers for Disease Control (CDC) conducted a survey in 2010 of the prevalence of depression. The statistics showed that nearly one in ten individuals in the United States suffered from depression during a one-year period of time. It is epidemic. The condition has been misunderstood for generations. And those who suffer often do so in silence. One day, we hear of a person we know who took his or her own life. Nobody had any idea.

I remember again my friend who observed, "The way things are going, if you aren't depressed there's something wrong with you." It was more than a year later that I received a phone call early one morning. I was informed that he and his wife were found in their farm home dead from a murder suicide. My heart ached! He was there for me as support, and I didn't recognize the seriousness of his own untreated depression.

Do you recognize depression as a serious health condition that needs to be diagnosed and treated whether in your family, church, and community? What role does religion have in addressing depression? Has religion been helpful or hurtful? Does religion shame the depressed for not having enough faith? Or does religion provide strong support and help for those who feel hopeless? Is there a depression support group in your church?

The times they are a changin'

But if you will not obey the Lord your God . . . The Lord will change the rain of your land into powder, and only dust shall come down upon you from the sky until you are destroyed. *Deuteronomy 28:15, 24*

Did I get your attention with this text? It is very harsh. Deuteronomy 28 describes the benefits (blessings) of following the laws of the Lord and the consequences (curses) of disobedience. The quoted text describes the environmental cost of disobedience. Now that's a picture of unwanted change!

In 1963 Bob Dylan captured the theme of the boomer generation in his song "The Times They Are a Changin.'" Since then have we seen changes! There was the civil rights movement, the women's movement, the environmental movement, Vietnam, the technology revolution, to name just a few. Change continues. What changes have you experienced and welcomed? What changes have been difficult for you and unwanted?

In his 2006 book *The Worst Hard Time*, Timothy Egan tells the untold story of those who survived the Great American Dust Bowl. Farming practices plowed up the western prairie from Texas to North Dakota in the 1920s. Times were good, the rains came, crops were plentiful, and money was being made hand over fist. But the soil was left exposed to the wind. When drought returned to the prairie, the winds blew the powered dry soil into toxic dust clouds. Breathing the dust was deadly. Dust pneumonia killed many children and adults. Crops failed year after year and hopes were crushed; it was the worst hard time.

Egan tells the story of Webster County Nebraska farmer Don Hartwell who kept a diary. On July 10, 1939, he made this entry: "The same clear, glaring sky & vicious blazing killing sun. Cane is about dead, corn is being damaged; it will soon be destroyed. Those who coined the phrase 'There's no place like Nebraska' wrote better than they thought. In Nebraska, you don't have to die to go to hell" (p. 300).

I am struck by how Hartwell and many like him actually experienced what Deuteronomy 28 described as an unwanted future. What caused this horrible catastrophe? Were humans responsible? The people on the prairie regarded themselves as Christians. It was difficult for them to believe that anything they did with farming caused such dust storms. But we know today that they were responsible. There are unwanted consequences when we unbalance nature's ecosystems, good Christians or not.

The times are a changin'. The climate is a changin'. Technology is a changin'. Life is constantly changin'. Ray's humor pictures hunters watching the geese fly south in an X formation instead of a V formation. They wonder, "Why does everything have to change?"

Where do you see God at work in these times that are a changin'? Change is inevitable. Each one of us can join together and be agents of desirable change to create a better future. What challenges do you see that must be overcome?

A welcoming church

Welcome one another, therefore, just as Christ has welcomed you, for the glory of God. *Romans 15:7*

I don't know of a church that doesn't claim to be friendly.

When we belong to a small group in a church with a mission that is important to us, we feel connected and valued as part of the group. If our church is small we feel welcome if we can fit in as part of the church family.

When I was serving as pastor in a parish, one year the evangelism committee decided to have a "perfect attendance Sunday." It sounded corny. But this approach was used as a way to encourage people who already belonged but who didn't attend worship often to come a particular Sunday.

Many families came that Sunday. One family that came expressed that they were anxious about coming to church otherwise, because people would ask embarrassing questions such as, "So, where have you been all these years?" or "My god, the world must be coming to an end for you to show up!"

Somehow people think they are funny when making such remarks. It usually isn't funny, it isn't friendly, and it isn't welcoming, either. So much for the perception of being a friendly church.

The good part of the evangelism strategy called "perfect attendance" Sunday was to create the message that if you hadn't been to worship for a long time, others would be there just like yourself, and you wouldn't be singled out for insensitive humor and criticism.

Ray's cartoon with the church sign makes me smile. We're trying to be as friendly as we say we are. So why not admit it? Let's say we are trying to be better.

How do you welcome the members who only occasionally attend? How do you welcome the stranger who is coming to check out your congregation?

At one point in my life I was new working as a chaplain, no longer a called pastor to a congregation. I went to visit churches in the area where I moved. It was summer, and I remember visiting several congregations. In most settings I walked in alone, received a bulletin, and sat down in the pew. I experienced no acknowledgment; no attempt was made to ask who I was. It was when I visited a congregation where people talked to me, that I considered attending again to worship.

We can miss seeing the stranger. How do you and members of your church "welcome one another . . . just as Christ has welcomed you, for the glory of God?"

Church socials

They devoted themselves to the apostles' teaching and fellowship, to the breaking of bread and the prayers. *Acts 2:42*

Christian community has been focused from the beginning on eating and drinking, fellowship, breaking of bread, and prayers.

Worship that centers around the Eucharist reminds us that the meaning of Jesus' life, death, and resurrection was communicated to his disciples gathered around a table eating and drinking.

So it is no surprise that church life also includes less formal meals. Historically they have been called church socials, potluck dinners, covered-dish suppers, Easter breakfasts, fellowship meals, funeral lunches, wedding dinners, lutefisk dinners, Lenten soup or fish dinners, and other excuses for eating together.

As poverty increased in many communities in recent years, churches have opened their doors to the homeless and others for weekly meals and fellowship.

What meals and fellowship events do you and your church have for members and/or others in your community?

Ray's cartoon of church mice having a strategic conversation about what kind of church to visit brings a smile. Churches with lots of potluck meals are good places to visit presuming leftovers are plentiful. The expression "poor as a church mouse" has a history from the days when a poor parish called a poor pastor and all the resources were utilized with nothing left for the church mouse. You were really poor if you as were poor as a church mouse.

Now I have some church mouse stories. Maybe you do too. One is my memory of the time when a church mouse walked slowly and quietly atop the altar rail as the pastor was preaching during Sunday worship. Needless to say it caused quite a stir. I also remember the time when a mouse ran down the aisle from the back of the church toward the front during a worship service. Scared to death, it ran up the pant leg of one of the seated parishioners. Luckily he was a farmer and knew how to deal with the situation. Grabbing his pant leg he got up. He limped down the aisle with his hand firmly grasping the mouse inside his pants. Now that was a sight to behold! But I don't have a story to add about a church mouse attending a church social in the fellowship hall after worship. Maybe you do?

Church socials are very important ways for people to be together and to build a sense of relationship and family. And a church mouse story sprinkled into the conversation can also generate a lot of laughter. Church socials are meant to be fun, building community.

Come Lord Jesus, protect us from church "mice" and let these hot dishes be free of norovirus. Amen (I tried to make this rhyme!)

Church of the Starbuck's™ coffee hour

The church coffee hour is one of those icons of many a church. "Why don't you stay for coffee after church so we can visit a while?" is a question that possibly should be added to the end of the worship liturgy. And all God's people, and even the other people, say, "Ya Sure!"

Ray Johnson captured the rise in the popularity of coffee shops with this cartoon. With his sense of humor he wondered what it would look like if a church adopted a popular coffee franchise as an attachment to the church. If you wondered the same thing, take a look.

In America we've now entered the age of "franchise heaven." Popular franchises and brands have popped up in every community, in every state, and even throughout the world wherever American brands and businesses exist. We can travel almost anywhere and "feel at home" if we enter a familiar brand of coffee shop, a familiar franchise brand of dining, a familiar name brand store, or a familiar name brand motel or hotel.

So what would happen if your church became known as the church of the Starbuck's coffee hour? Or if you are from Minnesota you might prefer to be the church of the Caribou™ coffee hour? Those of you whose church prefers a small business, local flavor that opposes the worldwide franchising trend, may say, "No, we are the church of the Sister Sludge coffee hour." We are a local church with a local ministry dedicated to our local community, keeping our money in local businesses like Sister Sludge, thank you!"

"Branding" as it is called, has risen to a sophisticated science aimed at influencing the behaviors of people. Faith communities and congregations are now using branding. The Evangelical Lutheran Church in America, the church body in which I am called to serve, uses "God's Work, Our Hands" as a mission statement and emblem of identity. Do you like being part of a community that engages God's work using our hands? If so, this is for you!

What brand, identity, logo, marker, or saying is used to communicate who your congregation is, what it is about, and what is important? Does your church have name recognition? What is your reputation? When visitors come to your church will they find it to be what is advertised?

A friend who once owned a Dairy Queen franchise™ told the story of listening to the local small town radio station in his place of business on a hot summer day. An advertisement by a hamburger chain promoting ice cream was played. Very soon after, a number of cars pulled in to his Dairy Queen. Why? When you think of ice cream, you think Dairy Queen, not a hamburger stand. That's how powerful branding is. Do people drive into your church when they hear a radio ad paid for by a different church? Interesting question!

Now I think I'll go have some Dairy Queen ice cream with my Caribou Coffee at the church picnic. Do you wanna come?

YOU ARE HEREBY CERTIFIED·HOMOGENIZED
DEMAGNETIZED, AFFIRMED, CONFIRMED, AND
STIGMATIZED AS A LUTHERAN, AND GRANTED
FULL PRIVILEGES TO MORE FULLY ENTER
INTO A LIFETIME OF STRUGGLE OF TRYING
TO FIND OUT WHAT THIS MIGHT MEAN.

Confirmed and homogenized

For those of us who are older Lutherans, confirmation was a ritual that carried a lot of stress and pressure. I can remember the practice of standing in front of the congregation the night before the Sunday of confirmation. We were asked questions from *Luther's Small Catechism* regarding the teachings of the church and also asked the familiar question: "What does this mean?" Of course, we were all asked to memorize the Commandments, the Creed, and the Lord's Prayer—plus what Luther said they meant.

Over my lifetime other approaches to confirmation were used. Memorizing was out. Let's try being relational and have experiences at retreats. When parents complained that the kids weren't learning the catechism like they had to, then a return to memorizing was tried. But teaching methods in schools were changing as well. Needless to say the ministry of the church leading to confirmation has had a varied trail of experimentation. Eventually among many Lutherans first communion was separated from the rite of confirmation and offered to younger children. Then confirmation became Affirmation of Baptism.

So how has all of this change in rites of passage worked out? Has it been good? Is it still a struggle?

Ray's cartoon reminds me of the pressures and expectations that accompanied the rite of confirmation. Ray shows in his cartoon what many a pastor may be thinking. I laugh out loud every time I see this.

I confess that when I think back on my confirmation I probably was certified, homogenized, affirmed, confirmed, and stigmatized. And I did enter into a lifetime of struggle. The only thing I missed was being demagnetized!

In the cartoon there is also a personal confession by the pastor who admits not figuring everything out yet. And in this confession lies the heart of what Ray and I talked about when we met as friends and brothers for our mutual support. The struggles of life do overwhelm. We both, in our different ways, bit the dust along the road of life. Depression, anxiety, grief and loss, and failure to achieve dreams were all very real experiences.

Pastors and other church workers continue the risk of burnout. The stresses of leadership, high expectations, and conflicting agendas all take a toll. In the old days, pastors were expected to be "good with the kids" and be "good" at teaching confirmation. A new bishop was elected at our synod convention years ago. During his address to the convention after being elected he said, "Well, the best part of this is that I won't need to teach confirmation anymore." All laughed! Many of the pastors definitely knew how he felt. And others criticized him for saying so.

How is the teaching and faith formation of the next generation going in your church and your family? What has been learned and what has been effective in helping children grow in their sense of belonging to the faith? Are young people still confirmed and homogenized today?

"I don't covet your house
or your wife, but I'd sure
like to have your pickup."

Coveting your neighbor's pickup

The Tenth Commandment: You shall not covet your neighbor's wife, or male or female slave, or ox, or donkey, or anything that belongs to your neighbor.

Luther's meaning: We are to fear and love God, so that we do not entice, force, or steal away from our neighbors their spouses, workers, or livestock, but instead urge them to stay and remain loyal to our neighbors. *Luther's Small Catechism* (contemporary translation by Timothy J. Wengert, Augsburg Fortress, 2001)

Yup, the house and wife are of no interest. But I sure do covet your new pickup! Most guys can relate to that. And maybe a few women, too.

The word *covet* isn't used much in daily life. But we know it means wanting something or even craving something. Young children may crave a candy bar their parent refused to buy and then decide to go back to the store when nobody is looking and take it. Now that moves us from just coveting to stealing—known as shoplifting—which isn't allowed by the Ten Commandments, either.

Maybe you've seen a popular bumper sticker that reads, "Yes it's my truck and NO you can't borrow it." This also illustrates a message delivered toward a behavior that's familiar.

So what do you covet or want or crave that someone else has?

Do you see the experiences of desire to be normal? Are they a problem? Do they lead us into temptation to steal?

Some of us have more problems with impulse control. We are tempted to buy something we really cannot afford. We may get ourselves into financial problems as a result. Others of us may be more cautious and critical of those whose desires run wild.

Whether it's radio, television, newspapers, or the internet using computers and cell phones, advertisers are everywhere tempting you and enticing you to desire the new pickup, a new boat, and a million things more.

How do you cope with this constant stream of messages that are designed to condition your mind and influence you?

Do you view advertising as a good and helpful flow of information to help you when shopping? Or is it a problem that causes you stress when you know you can't afford any of the items being advertised and sold?

Have you thought that maybe our way of life has been built on the foundation of tempting our desires to covet what is our neighbors? It used to be called, "keeping up with the Joneses."

Maybe this is why teaching children Luther's catechism and in this case especially the Tenth Commandment is so difficult. I'm still thinking about that pickup.

Shelters

> Is not this the fast that I choose: to loose the bonds of injustice, to undo the thongs of the yoke, to let the oppressed go free, and to break every yoke? Is it not to share your bread with the hungry, and bring the homeless poor into your house; when you see the naked, to cover them, and not to hide yourself from your own kin? *Isaiah 58:6-7*

The prophet Isaiah reminds us that performing religious rituals such as fasting are not enough to please God. Fasting includes giving bread to the hungry and bringing the homeless into one's home. True religion is caring for those in need.

Ray's drawing sets forth a contrast we see in our communities today. Wealth and poverty sit side by side. It's nothing new.

In 1908 a wealthy Swedish newspaper entrepreneur, Swan Turnblad, built a mansion for his family in what is now south Minneapolis, Minnesota. He wanted to impress and show his wealth, according to the history of the mansion. And he did!

A few years later in 1917 Norwegian Lutheran immigrant churches were facing a problem of elderly poor who had no place to live. Land was secured across the street from the Swedish Turnblad mansion, and the churches built a home for homeless Norwegian immigrants called the Ebenezer Home. Income disparity and homelessness lived side by side.

In December 1929 at the time of the stock market crash, the Turnblad mansion was donated to become a Swedish cultural center. No longer would it be a lavish home for a wealthy family. Ebenezer still cares for the needs of the poor and homeless in the same neighborhood. Today its mission relies on government-subsidized affordable housing and Medicare and Medicaid to pay for nursing care and other medical costs.

A woman, whose father once lived at Ebenezer Care Center, told us that ending up homeless and living on the street was her mother's greatest fear. As a young woman, she decided to face her mother's fear. So she quit her job, sold her possessions, and lived in poverty on the streets of San Francisco. "I wanted to see what was like," she said. "I discovered the most difficult part of the experience was the lack of privacy. On the street and in the shelters, privacy was nil." She missed her privacy more than she missed money and other possessions. Now seeing what it was like to be poor and homeless, she knew that she could handle anything. She conquered the greatest fear that consumed her mother.

Have you ever been homeless at some time in your life? If you are fortunate to be among those with "tax shelters for the already lavishly homed," can you imagine being homeless?

Isaiah 58 teaches that caring for the hungry, poor, and homeless is the fast (act of worship) that God approves. This challenge will always be with us. How do you and your faith community care for those who face hardship, are homeless, and in need?

Grace happens

The law indeed was given through Moses; grace and truth came through Jesus Christ. *John 1:17*

All who knew Ray Johnson will never forget his bumper sticker: GRACE HAPPENS.

This message was core to his faith and courage. It is a message that resonates with anyone who has struggled and faced failure, hopelessness, depression, anxiety, despair, grief, or loss.

The old legalism is still in the background, part of history, still condemning us. We were never good enough, smart enough, caring enough, virtuous enough. We disappointed our parents, our teachers, our friends, our employers. It's what Martin Luther called the first purpose of the law, to condemn us as sinners.

Whether you call it sin, failure, imperfection, or defect, every person with a conscience knows something of the experience of disgrace.

Grace is God's second chance. *Grace Happens* every time we get up and start over. It is never deserved or earned. We cannot let condemnation remain and ruin our lives. It must be repealed, removed, and overcome. And so it is through *grace*.

As a young pastor many years ago I was called to visit a young man living in a group home. He wanted to talk to a pastor. When I arrived, I found a young man with developmental disabilities and also a sense of struggle. That's why I was called. He had questions about religion, he said. Eventually I asked him if he had a favorite Bible verse. Immediately he said, "The wages of sin is death!" I was stunned. Why would such a vulnerable young man choose these words as his favorite Bible verse? Then I realized, as a child and young person with his disabilities, he suffered ridicule, rejection, and mocking from his peers. He was regarded as different. I will never know all he suffered, but I now knew why this passage was his favorite. It described his life experience of condemnation. He was a "bad boy!"

I asked if he knew the rest of the Bible verse he quoted. He said, "No." So I took his Bible and found Roman 6:23. "For the wages of sin is death," I read. Do you see what follows, I asked? I read, "but the free gift of God is eternal life in Christ Jesus our Lord." It was news to him.

It's news to many of us that *Grace Happens* as a free gift of God without our deserving or help. Healing in physical and spiritual care comes to all as grace, forgiveness, unconditional love, and compassion. Grace is good medicine. We all need more of it.

History of Ray's cartoons

Ray's cartoons and illustrations have been published many places over several decades of his lifetime. His cartoons were found in *The Lutheran* and *Lutheran Partners* magazines, publications of the Lutheran Church in America (LCA), and also in publications of the Evangelical Lutheran Church in America (ELCA).

In an interview with *The Lutheran* (April 2003) Ray is quoted: "We often take ourselves too seriously and need humor to jolt us out of our rigid tendencies." He went on to say that he started cartooning as a survival skill during tedious synodical meetings: "I don't have the personality type to sit through that tedium. I'd pass my cartoons down the table, and they'd make their way through the convention." That's what many pastors and lay delegates to synod conventions remember about Ray. He would tickle our funny bones during boring and even intense discussions.

The *Metro Lutheran,* with primary circulation in the Twin Cities of Minnesota, featured his cartoons for many years. His cartoons also found their way into local Minnesota newspapers such as in New York Mills and Fergus Falls, and in the White Bear Press, where his cartoons were featured weekly until his untimely death. Ray also joined the Edina Miniature Yacht Club and salted their membership publication *Sail & Scale* with his cartoons.

The consultant firm *Change Making Systems* led by John Johnson (no family relationship to Ray) partnered with Ray Johnson to use his illustrations and cartoons for training and to express appreciation to the firm's clients. John Johnson reports, "Ray's cartoons are hanging on the walls of many corporate offices and nonprofit organizational offices throughout the country, with clients whom I have worked with over the years." John Johnson remembers this about Ray: "He embraced so many opposites. He was almost always in pain as he would celebrate, have fun, and enjoy life. The coexistence of joy and pain in him made him very influential, genuine, an out-of-the-box guy whose work could touch you deeply and twist something familiar into a new way of seeing." John remembers, "I would send holiday greeting prints every year to clients, especially created for them by Ray. They would almost always frame them and display them in their homes or offices. Christians, Jews, or atheists, all of them loved his work." He continued, "We had so many dreams for what we were going to do next when he unexpectedly died." Still feeling the loss John added, "It's not what we had dreamed about, but I'm glad you are doing this book to honor him and what he meant to many of us."

Pastor Bill Strom, Ray's friend and seminary classmate, reported that Ray Johnson's cartoon work appeared often in Pete Einstein books and his large *Healthy Congregations* workshop training material. Other books in which his cartoons were published include: *A Door Set Open*, the Alban Institute, 2010; *Healthy Congregations, A Systems Approach,* the Alban Institute, 1996; *How Your Church Family Works,* the Alban Institute, 1993. The one large work featuring a number of Ray's cartoons is called *Healthy Congregations Facilitator Manual* by Peter L. Steinke, published in 1999.

Other places and publications not mentioned here no doubt have been sprinkled with Ray's cartoons and drawing through the years.

IDENTIFY THE LUTHERAN